MW01234482

STORYTELLER

A Creative Writing Journal And Guide To Unlock Your Inner Wordsmith

Copyright © 2022 by Sarah Hickner

All rights reserved.

No portion of this book may be reproduced in any form without written permission from the publisher or author, except as permitted by U.S. copyright law.

Welcome to your new journal!

Here are just a few of the things you'll find here:

- Journal prompts (ok that one's obvious)
- Writing tips your teachers (probably) never told you
- Fun pages to kickstart creativity
- Doodle pages
- Block by block building of your short story
- Blank pages to let loose and run like a wild mustang
- and other random fun things!
- Don't worry - there will be absolutely no sentence diagramming here.

Let's Go!

One more thing before you dive in...
You have received one of the very first
printings of this journal! (So cool, right?!).
Will you do me the biggest favor, and leave
a review on Amazon? Reviews will help
other people find this journal so they can
enjoy it too.
Thanks!

You can use the bottom half of this page to
doodle. I'd draw a pony, but that's just me.
~Sarah

"It's none of their business that you have to learn to write. Let them think you were born that way."
—Ernest Hemingway

ALL ABOUT ME

My name is
_____

This is a picture of me!

I am _____ years old.

I live in _____

When I'm not writing, I like to _____
_____

This is my favorite book!

If you find this book, please return it! Here's how you can get it back to me:

"I rode a thousand horses before I ever put my foot in a stirrup, all thanks to books."
Sarah Hickner

READING LOG

BOOK: _____

AUTHOR: _____

START DATE: _____ END DATE: _____

BOOK: _____

AUTHOR: _____

START DATE: _____ END DATE: _____

BOOK: _____

AUTHOR: _____

START DATE: _____ END DATE: _____

BOOK: _____

AUTHOR: _____

START DATE: _____ END DATE: _____

BOOK: _____

AUTHOR: _____

START DATE: _____ END DATE: _____

I ♡ Stories

Writers are readers. Write about a book or story that inspires you.

_____
_____
_____
_____
_____
_____
_____
_____
_____
_____
_____
_____
_____
_____
_____
_____
_____
_____
_____
_____
_____
_____
_____
_____
_____

New things you'd like to try

Throughout the journal, you'll see pages titled, "Try Something New Review." Take some time to brainstorm new things you'd like to try. It could be as simple as baking something you've never baked before, painting rocks, or even jogging an entire mile without stopping.

- ☐ _____
- ☐ _____
- ☐ _____
- ☐ _____
- ☐ _____
- ☐ _____
- ☐ _____
- ☐ _____
- ☐ _____
- ☐ _____
- ☐ _____

It's important to try new things. It actually helps you become a better writer because you can authentically describe your experiences!

TRY SOMETHING NEW REVIEW!

STRETCH YOUR COMFORT ZONE, EXPERIENCE
SOMETHING NEW, AND WRITE ABOUT IT HERE!

NEW THING: DATE:

WHAT DID YOU HOPE TO   WHAT WAS YOUR ATTITUDE
ACCOMPLISH OR LEARN?   LIKE GOING INTO THE
                                                   EXPERIENCE?

WHAT WAS THE HARDEST PART   WHAT WAS THE BEST PART?
OF THE NEW EXPERIENCE?

WILL YOU DO THIS AGAIN?   WHAT'S THE NEXT NEW
IF SO, WHEN?   THING YOU'D LIKE TO TRY?

KNOW & GROW

List 5 things you are good at.

1

2

3

4

5

List 5 things you'd like to learn or get better at.

1

2

3

4

5

DOODLE PAGE

fun

Would you rather be a world-famous author, actor, or artist? Choose one, and write a story about your dream achievement in that role.

_____
_____
_____
_____
_____
_____
_____
_____
_____
_____
_____
_____
_____
_____
_____
_____
_____
_____
_____
_____
_____
_____
_____

Make a playlist of songs that make you smile!

My Favorite Day

Draw a picture of your favorite day – real or imagined! This will be the first step to writing your own story.

My Favorite Day

It's time to start telling your story! Let's start with the basics. Think of your favorite day while filling out the spaces below...

What made it so special?

Who was with you?

What time of day and year did it happen?

Where did it take place?

Why was it important?

Describe
"My Favorite Day"
with your five senses.

This will help the story come alive to the reader.

looks	feels	smells	sounds	tastes

Storyteller

"My Favorite Day"
Parts of the story
Take some time to identify these three elements of your story. Write yours below.

Conflict - this is the struggle you are working to overcome. It could be convincing your parents to let you have a dog, having a hard time learning to swim, or overcoming a fear. The conflict is the core of the story.

Climax - this is the point of greatest tension where your conflict gets the most difficult - your parents are saying you most likely can't get a dog, you feel like you'll never figure out swimming and you want to give up, the thing you fear the most starts to happen.

Resolution - the end of the story where the conflict is resolved - you get a puppy! (or maybe a fish as a compromise), you victoriously swim an entire lap, you faced your fear and lived to tell the story!

"My Favorite Day"

Are you ready? I believe you are! Using all the things you've prepared, it's time to piece it together and write your story.

DOODLE PAGE

smile

Poetry Corner

Cinquain

A Cinquain is a five-lined poem. It is easy to write, and fun to read!

_____
Line 1: a noun (what the poem is about)

_____ _____
Line 2: 2 adjectives that describe Line 1

_____ _____ _____
Line 3: 3 -ing action verbs related to Line 1

____ ____ ____ ____
Line 4: 4 words to make a phrase or sentence that relates to Line 1

_____
Line 5: 1 synonym for Line 1

example: Horse
Handsome bay
Nuzzling, trotting, jumping
Makes my heart happy
Silas

"Show Don't Tell"

In the writing world there is a saying, "show don't tell." It refers to using descriptive words to create an image of the story in the reader's mind instead of simply telling it. I'll use this page to give examples, and on the next page you can practice!

Tell: The horse was nervous.

show:

The mare's body trembled as a white rim appeared around her eyes.

Tell: Silas was hungry.

show:

Silas pawed at his feed bucket, banging the plastic, as he anticipated dinner.

Tell: It is hot outside.

show:

The pavement burned my feet and sweat trickled between my shoulder blades.

Tell: It was early morning.

show:

The sun was low on the horizon.

Tell: I was so annoyed.

show:

I grit my teeth together, slowly breathing to keep from yelling.

"Show Don't Tell"

Your turn!

Tell: The dog was excited!

show:

Tell: Clyde was thirsty.

show:

Tell: I am confused.

show:

Tell: It is late afternoon.

show:

Tell: I was hungry.

show:

Come up with a story about this picture.

What is his name? What is he chasing?

_____

_____

_____

_____

_____

_____

_____

_____

_____

_____

_____

_____

_____

_____

_____

_____

_____

Design a Book Cover

Don't forget to add your name as the author!

EXPERIENCE YOUR WORLD

List some of your favorite things, and write about
how you experience them through your senses!
(I'll do one as an example)

SMELLS

- [ ] horses - peppermint breath
- [ ] _____
- [ ] _____
- [ ] _____
- [ ] _____
- [ ] _____

SOUNDS

- [ ] _____
- [ ] _____
- [ ] _____
- [ ] _____
- [ ] _____
- [ ] _____

FEELS

- [ ] _____
- [ ] _____
- [ ] _____
- [ ] _____
- [ ] _____
- [ ] _____

Writing with Strong Verbs

A verb is the action word in a sentence: run, walk, think, talk, sit, stand, go. Most people write using simple verbs, and then add something called an adverb to describe it: run fast, walk slow, talk loud.

One technique for improving creative writing is using strong verbs. A strong verb conveys the picture or feeling without needing descriptive words: sprint, trudge, yell.

Examples:

weak: Gideon ran really fast.
strong: Gideon sprinted.

weak: Waylon stepped quickly into the mud puddle.
strong: Waylon plunged into the mud puddle.

Practice
Rewrite these sentences and make them better using strong verbs.

The boy walked excitedly down the path.

_____

The girl ate ice cream.

_____

Writing with Strong Verbs

more practice!

Flip back through the journal and find sentences with weak verbs. Copy them into the box, and then rewrite using strong verbs.

● ○ ○
weak

○───────────────────────────────────○

○───────────────────────────────────○

strong

○───────────────────────────────────○

○───────────────────────────────────○

● ○ ○
weak

○───────────────────────────────────○

○───────────────────────────────────○

strong

○───────────────────────────────────○

○───────────────────────────────────○

● ○ ○
weak

○───────────────────────────────────○

○───────────────────────────────────○

strong

○───────────────────────────────────○

○───────────────────────────────────○

DOODLE PAGE

persist

What is happening?
Are they playing?
Fighting? Why is the poor
bunny a victim? Or is the
bunny actually evil? It's
your story to tell...

_____

_____

_____

_____

_____

_____

_____

_____

_____

_____

_____

_____

_____

_____

_____

_____

_____

_____

_____

_____

_____

_____

Life isn't all sunshine and rainbows. Write about a tough day you recently had.

List Your Favorite Snacks

Do you like healthy snacks? Sweet snacks?
Chips? Or chocolate dipped pretzels?

1. $\longleftrightarrow$

2. $\longleftrightarrow$

3. $\longleftrightarrow$

4. $\longleftrightarrow$

5. $\longleftrightarrow$

6. $\longleftrightarrow$

7. $\longleftrightarrow$

Thinking about the tough day
you recently wrote about, what
was a good thing that came
from it?

_____

_____

_____

_____

_____

_____

_____

_____

_____

_____

_____

_____

_____

_____

_____

_____

_____

_____

_____

_____

_____

_____

_____

"Reading is essential for those who seek to rise above the ordinary." - Jim Rohn

READING LOG

BOOK: _____

AUTHOR: _____

START DATE: _____ END DATE: _____

BOOK: _____

AUTHOR: _____

START DATE: _____ END DATE: _____

BOOK: _____

AUTHOR: _____

START DATE: _____ END DATE: _____

BOOK: _____

AUTHOR: _____

START DATE: _____ END DATE: _____

BOOK: _____

AUTHOR: _____

START DATE: _____ END DATE: _____

Make a playlist of songs that inspire you!

A Lesson I Learned

Draw a picture from a day you learned an important lesson! It could be something like learning to not give up, learning to forgive your friend, or learning to ride a bike!

A Lesson I Learned

It's time to start telling another story! Let's start with the basics. Imagine a lesson you've learned...

What was the lesson?

Who was with you?

What time of day and year did it happen?

Where did it take place?

Why was it important?

Describe
"A Lesson I Learned"
with your five senses.

This will help the story come alive for the reader.

looks	feels	smells	sounds	tastes

"A Lesson I Learned"

PARTS OF THE STORY

Take some time to identify these three elements of your story. Write them below.

Conflict - this is the struggle you are working to overcome. It could be convincing your parents to let you have a dog, having a hard time learning to swim, or overcoming a fear. The conflict is the core of the story.

Climax - this is the point of greatest tension where your conflict gets the most difficult - your parents are saying you most likely can't get a dog, you feel like you'll never figure out swimming and you want to give up, the thing you fear the most starts to happen.

Resolution - the end of the story where the conflict is resolved - you get a puppy! (or maybe a fish as a compromise), you victoriously swim an entire lap, you faced your fear and lived to tell the story!

"A Lesson I Learned"

Are you ready? I believe you are! Using all the things you've prepared, it's time to write your story.

_____

_____

_____

_____

_____

_____

_____

_____

_____

_____

_____

_____

_____

_____

_____

_____

_____

Storyteller

DOODLE PAGE

Learn

Write a letter to either your favorite pet or your dream pet.

_____

_____

_____

_____

_____

_____

_____

_____

_____

_____

_____

_____

_____

_____

_____

_____

_____

_____

_____

_____

_____

_____

_____

Write a quote you love in the center box. Feel free to color or decorate it!

DOODLE PAGE

dream

If you could go anywhere in the world, where would you go and what would you do when you get there?

_____
_____
_____
_____
_____
_____
_____
_____
_____
_____
_____
_____
_____
_____
_____
_____
_____
_____
_____
_____
_____

TRY SOMETHING NEW REVIEW!

STRETCH YOUR COMFORT ZONE, EXPERIENCE
SOMETHING NEW, AND WRITE ABOUT IT HERE!

NEW THING: DATE:

WHAT DID YOU HOPE TO   WHAT WAS YOUR ATTITUDE
ACCOMPLISH OR LEARN?   LIKE GOING INTO THE
                                                     EXPERIENCE?

WHAT WAS THE HARDEST PART   WHAT WAS THE BEST PART?
OF THE NEW EXPERIENCE?

WILL YOU DO THIS AGAIN?   WHAT'S THE NEXT NEW
IF SO, WHEN?   THING YOU'D LIKE TO TRY?

Scrambled

Unscramble the words, then draw a line to match the word with its definition.

BRVE _____   A word that describes a noun.

Vjadeitce _____   A word that describes a verb, adjective, or other adverb.

nnuo _____   A word used to join words or groups of words. Examples: And, or

soonppreiit _____   A type of word that replaces a noun, such as 'she,' 'he,' 'you,' 'them,' and 'this.'

budrea _____   A word used to describe an action.

jcutcnnnioo _____   A naming word for a person, an animal, a place, a thing, or idea.

nurpoon _____   A word used to show the relation of one thing to another. Examples: about, below, in

(answers in back of book)

Poetry Corner

Haiku

A haiku is an unrhymed three-line poem. The traditional pattern in English is to write the first and last lines with five syllables each, and the middle line with seven syllables.

Line 1: 5 syllables
Line 2: 7 syllables
Line 3: 5 syllables

example:
Throw the ball to first.
Ball beats the runner. He's out.
Runner batted in.

Try writing a couple Haikus of your own!

DOODLE PAGE

believe

Using Words for Good

"Pretend that everyone has a sign around their neck that says make me feel important."

~Mary Kay Ash

THINGS PEOPLE HAVE SAID THAT MADE YOU FEEL IMPORTANT

1. ....

2. ....

3. ....

THINGS YOU CAN SAY TO OTHERS TO MAKE THEM FEEL IMPORANT

1. ....

2. ....

3. ....

WHO WOULD YOU LOVE TO ENCOURAGE?

DOODLE PAGE

Work Hard

 # My Goals

THINGS I WANT TO LEARN

plan it out

THINGS I WANT TO ACHIEVE

THINGS I WANT TO DO

OTHER GOALS

TRY SOMETHING NEW REVIEW!

STRETCH YOUR COMFORT ZONE, EXPERIENCE SOMETHING NEW, AND WRITE ABOUT IT HERE!

NEW THING: DATE:

WHAT DID YOU HOPE TO ACCOMPLISH OR LEARN?

WHAT WAS YOUR ATTITUDE LIKE GOING INTO THE EXPERIENCE?

WHAT WAS THE HARDEST PART OF THE NEW EXPERIENCE?

WHAT WAS THE BEST PART?

WILL YOU DO THIS AGAIN? IF SO, WHEN?

WHAT'S THE NEXT NEW THING YOU'D LIKE TO TRY?

Story Ideas

Write ideas for stories you'd love to write!

Create a Character

From the clothes she wears to the way she smells, create your very own story character. Add hair, eyes, clothes, and whatever else you want!

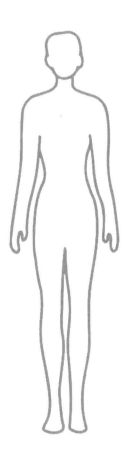

Create a Character

Answer these questions about your character.

Name: _____

Age: _____

Favorite color:_____

Favorite food: _____

Favorite animal: _____

Is she an extrovert or introvert? _____

What does she smell like? _____

What's her biggest pet peeve?_____

What makes her feel alive? _____

What makes her smile?_____

What is her biggest fear? _____

If she could give one piece of advice, what would it be?_____

What's her dream?_____

Describe her family situation (married? single? siblings? kids?):_____

_____

STOP What you're doing. Assess the room using all your senses.

What do you see?

What do you feel against your skin?

What do you smell?

What do you hear?

What do you taste?

What do you feel with your extended senses? (think of the energy in the room)

List your Favorite Character Names

females   males

_____   _____

_____   _____

_____   _____

_____   _____

_____   _____

_____   _____

_____   _____

_____   _____

"The more that you read, the more things you will know. The more that you learn, the more places you'll go." - Dr. Seuss

READING LOG

BOOK: _____

AUTHOR: _____

START DATE: _____ END DATE: _____

BOOK: _____

AUTHOR: _____

START DATE: _____ END DATE: _____

BOOK: _____

AUTHOR: _____

START DATE: _____ END DATE: _____

BOOK: _____

AUTHOR: _____

START DATE: _____ END DATE: _____

BOOK: _____

AUTHOR: _____

START DATE: _____ END DATE: _____

Poetry Corner
Acrostic

Acrostic poems are simple and fun! You choose something you want to write about (I'll choose "Silas"), then write the word vertically.
Using the letters from your word as a starting place, write a word or sentence to describe your subject.

example: "Silas"

Stoic unless he's spooking at a log

Irritable when I groom him

Lazy when we're in the ring

Acrobatic when he doesn't get out enough

Special to me

I did the sentence version because it made me laugh! Here is a version with just a word:

"Silas"

Stoic

Irritable

Lazy

Acrobatic

Special

Poetry Corner
Acrostic

Your turn!
Write your own acrostic poem (or five).
Add a photo or illustration if you want.

Come up with a story about this picture. What are they looking at? Do they know each other? Where are they?

_____
_____
_____
_____
_____
_____
_____
_____
_____
_____
_____
_____
_____
_____
_____
_____
_____
_____
_____
_____

Create a Character

From the clothes he wears to the way he smells, create your very own story character. Add hair, eyes, clothes, and whatever else you want!

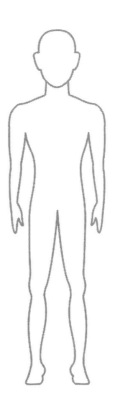

Create a Character

Answer these questions about your character.

Name: _____

Age: _____

Favorite color:_____

Favorite food: _____

Favorite animal: _____

Is he an extrovert or introvert? _____

What does he smell like? _____

What's his biggest pet peeve? _____

What makes him feel alive?_____

What makes him smile?_____

What is his biggest fear? _____

If he could give one piece of advice, what would it be?_____

What's his dream? _____

Describe his family situation (married? single? siblings? kids?):   _____

_____

Create a Character

Maybe this one is another person or maybe this character is an animal or a talking toy! The page is blank so you can create whatever your mind can conceive.

Create a Character

Answer these questions about your character.

Name: _____

Age: _____

Favorite color: _____

Favorite food: _____

Favorite animal: _____

Is it an extrovert or introvert? _____

What does it smell like? _____

What's its biggest pet peeve? _____

What makes it feel alive? _____

What makes it smile? _____

What is its biggest fear? _____

If it could give one piece of advice, what would it be? _____

What's its dream? _____

Describe its family situation (married? single? siblings? kids?): _____

_____

LET'S TALK ABOUT IT!

Dialogue can really bring a story to life. It's the difference between telling your reader what happened, and bringing them into the conversation.

Check it out: No dialogue

Joey asked if I wanted coffee. I wasn't sure what to get, so he picked something for me.

Dialogue

"Hey, Sarah!" Joey's deep voice startled me. "I'm running into the coffee shop. Want anything?"
"Um," I racked my brain.
"Want me to just pick something for you?" he asked with an understanding grin.
"Yes, please!"

Your turn! I'll give you one to start out:

Katie invited me to the fair, but I couldn't go.

Dialogue

This one's all on you. You can do it!

Dialogue

Choose a story from your story ideas page or something totally new – it's your journal after all.

Title:_____

Draw a picture from the story to help your brain start imagining all the details. Consider including some of the characters you've created!

Title: _____

It's time to start telling your story! Let's start with the basics.

What was the event?

Who was there?

What time of day and year did it happen?

Where did it take place?

Why was it important?

Describe your story with your five senses.

This will help the story come alive for the reader.

looks	feels	smells	sounds	tastes

Title:_____

PARTS OF THE STORY

Take some time to identify these three elements of your story.

Conflict - this is the struggle you are working to overcome. It could be convincing your parents to let you have a dog, having a hard time learning to swim, or overcoming a fear. The conflict is the core of the story.

Climax - this is the point of greatest tension where your conflict gets the most difficult - your parents are saying you most likely can't get a dog, you feel like you'll never figure out swimming and you want to give up, the thing you fear the most starts to happen.

Resolution - the end of the story where the conflict is resolved - you get a puppy! (or maybe a fish as a compromise), you victoriously swim an entire lap, you faced your fear and lived to tell the story!

Title: _____

Are you ready? I believe you are! Using all
the things you've prepared, it's time to
write your story.

_____

_____

_____

_____

_____

_____

_____

_____

_____

_____

_____

_____

_____

_____

_____

_____

DOODLE PAGE

Help Others

IMAGINE YOU'RE A FISH IN A BOWL. WHAT DO YOU THINK ABOUT ALL DAY? ARE YOU FRIENDS WITH THE OTHER FISH?

TRY SOMETHING NEW REVIEW!

STRETCH YOUR COMFORT ZONE, EXPERIENCE
SOMETHING NEW, AND WRITE ABOUT IT HERE!

NEW THING: DATE:

WHAT DID YOU HOPE TO
ACCOMPLISH OR LEARN?

WHAT WAS YOUR ATTITUDE
LIKE GOING INTO THE
EXPERIENCE?

WHAT WAS THE HARDEST PART
OF THE NEW EXPERIENCE?

WHAT WAS THE BEST PART?

WILL YOU DO THIS AGAIN?
IF SO, WHEN?

WHAT'S THE NEXT NEW
THING YOU'D LIKE TO TRY?

5 THINGS THAT MAKE YOU SMILE

THANK YOU

Write a thank-you note to someone who has encouraged or inspired you. Then rewrite it on a notecard or tear it out of the journal and send it to him or her!

DOODLE PAGE

Grow

Tell a little story about these treats or the person eating them!

_____
_____
_____
_____
_____
_____
_____
_____
_____
_____
_____
_____
_____
_____
_____
_____
_____
_____

cut THAT out

Did you know that the word 'that' is often unnecessary? To prove my point, see what happens when you cut the first 'that' out of the previous sentence. Sometimes it contributes to the sentence, and sometimes it doesn't.

Decide if 'that' is needed in the following sentences.

	is it needed?	
That car is fast.	**yes**	**no**
I love that the dog is spotted.	**yes**	**no**
Let's get ice cream from that corner store.	**yes**	**no**
She said that they would meet us soon.	**yes**	**no**

(answer in back of book)

TITLE _____

or

If you could choose, would you rather ride
a dragon or a griffin?

Write about it! What adventures would you go on?

_____

_____

_____

_____

_____

_____

_____

_____

_____

_____

_____

_____

_____

_____

_____

_____

_____

_____

_____

_____

Becoming a Great Writer

Something they don't always tell you in school (or maybe they tell you, but I didn't hear), is the best books have been written and rewritten, fixed, read, and fixed some more.

> **WE CALL THIS PROCESS "REVISION."**

It's quite a process!

When I started writing for other people, I wanted the first version to be perfect. In fact, I was convinced it was already a masterpiece! Newsflash to my past self: It was not even close to a masterpiece. I might even call it bad.

Now, I love revising! It's so fun to see your work evolve.

Look back into some of the journal entries or stories you've written, and use the next page and a half to rewrite all or part of one. You may cut out ~~extra~~ words, use stronger verbs, or see ~~that~~ you were "telling" the story but now you can "show" it with your words.

_____

_____

_____

_____

_____

_____

_____

Practice

TRY SOMETHING NEW REVIEW!

STRETCH YOUR COMFORT ZONE, EXPERIENCE
SOMETHING NEW, AND WRITE ABOUT IT HERE!

NEW THING: DATE:

WHAT DID YOU HOPE TO
ACCOMPLISH OR LEARN?

WHAT WAS YOUR ATTITUDE
LIKE GOING INTO THE
EXPERIENCE?

WHAT WAS THE HARDEST PART
OF THE NEW EXPERIENCE?

WHAT WAS THE BEST PART?

WILL YOU DO THIS AGAIN?
IF SO, WHEN?

WHAT'S THE NEXT NEW
THING YOU'D LIKE TO TRY?

Come up with a story about this picture.

Is it her dog? Why are they hugging?

_____

_____

_____

_____

_____

_____

_____

_____

_____

_____

_____

_____

_____

_____

_____

_____

_____

MY FAVORITES

What was your favorite activity from the journal?

Which pages are you most proud of?

What surprised you from the journal?

Did you or will you share some of your work with a teacher, friend, or parent?

What are your plans to keep growing as a writer?

Draw or write something that makes you smile :)

About the Author
(that's you)

Insert or draw a pic of yourself here

name _____

Tell the world about you:

_____
_____
_____
_____
_____
_____
_____
_____

Enjoy some blank pages - no rules or expectations!
Just have fun!

Did you write a story, journal entry, or poem that you're super proud of? I'd love to see it! Email it to me (Sarah) at StoriesFromTheBarnAisle@gmail.com

If you loved this journal, do me the biggest favor and leave a review on Amazon!

More from Sarah Hickner

In Sarah's debut book, she shares five hilarious true stories from her adventures with horses. It will leave you craving more horsehair in your life!

Available in paperback, ebook, and audio!

Do you love horses?
Do you love to write about them?
Then this journal is for you! It was created for the horse-obsessed people of the world, with an extra focus on learning to write epic short stories. But there's so much more than just story writing.

No real horse experience is required to enjoy this journal!

FREE Short Story!

Sarah and her fiancé are back home for a couple of weeks for a very special occasion — their wedding. But will an accident with the beautiful steed Joey is supposed to ride on their wedding day ruin all her little girl dreams?

For your free short story and updates on Sarah's book releases, sign up for her monthly newsletter at www.LiveRideLearn.com/freeshortstory

Answer Key

Scrambled

Unscramble the words, then draw a line to match the word with its definition.

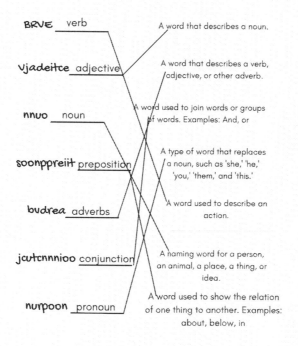

BRVE ___verb___

Vjadeitce ___adjective___

nnuo ___noun___

soonppreiit ___preposition___

budrea ___adverbs___

jcutcnnnioo ___conjunction___

nurpoon ___pronoun___

A word that describes a noun.

A word that describes a verb, adjective, or other adverb.

A word used to join words or groups of words. Examples: And, or

A type of word that replaces a noun, such as 'she,' 'he,' 'you,' 'them,' and 'this.'

A word used to describe an action.

A naming word for a person, an animal, a place, a thing, or idea.

A word used to show the relation of one thing to another. Examples: about, below, in

cut THAT out

Decide if 'that' is needed in the following sentences.

is it needed?

That car is fast. **(yes)** no

I love that the dog is spotted. **(yes)** no

Let's get ice cream from that corner store. **(yes)** no

She said that they would meet us soon. yes **(no)**

Made in the USA
Middletown, DE
18 August 2022

70646847R00077